Adam Crothers

Several Deer

CARCANET

First published in Great Britain in 2016 by Carcanet Press Limited
Alliance House, 30 Cross Street, Manchester, M2 7AQ
www.carcanet.co.uk / info@carcanet.co.uk

Typeset by Luke Allan in Sentinel.

The publisher acknowledges financial assistance from Arts Council
England.

A CIP catalogue record for this book is available from the British
Library, ISBN 978 1 78410 244 9

Adam Crothers was born in Belfast in 1984. He lives in Cambridge, where he completed a PhD in English at Girton College in 2010; he works as a library assistant, literary critic, and teacher.

Acknowledgements are due to the following publications, in which a number of these poems, some in earlier versions, previously appeared: *Antiphon, The Apple Anthology* (Nine Arches, 2013), *Blackbox Manifold, Ducts, Eborakon, Five Poetry Journal, The Literateur, The Mays, New Poetries VI* (Carcanet, 2015), *PN Review, Poetry Proper, The Stinging Fly, Wordlegs*. Many thanks to Rebecca Watts for her often blunt advice on sequencing and edits. All remaining aesthetic errors result from her failure to be sufficiently persuasive.

Adam Crothers

Several Deer

For Sabrina,

with many thanks and every

good wish.

[signature]

14 . 9 . 2017

Contents

———————————————————————————— **I**

———————————————————————————— **II**

III

For my mother

I

*Sing it. 'Tis no matter how it be in tune,
so it make noise enough.*

My Usual Flair

How can you call me a misogynist? My mother was a woman-
hater and I must at all costs rebel. When in a Roman

I do as girls do. Something about coming out of my shell.
Something about crying for joy at last, at last. Some hustle.

This wassail is for ballast, without which the surface
and the low point would meet. 'Welcome,' one says, 'to the circus,

sourface.' All that inclusiveness! I'd finally start getting fit.
Now, if only dropping a beat meant omitting it.

Now let the sins of the son be visited upon the father. Every son,
but my father specifically. Such is the work that heaven's done:

its bodies and their accusations. Sweet black angels, bats
make the air all quotation as I move to recast

their flawless punctuation as halting semicolons.
Here is your moment of uplift; now send in the clowns.

Blues for Kaki King

If I could get these six strings working they still wouldn't work on you.
I'm entitled to exit at any point and everybody's glad when I do.

I have never listened to 'Wild Thing' and felt sorry for myself.
Thin cuts of wild thing fall off the freezer shelf.

Now we're going to do a cheer starting way way back at the back
of the room and moving to the front in an approximation of Barack

Obama's attack on all that his great nation holds dear. I hit
the road, Jack. I hit several deer. I listen to the hits. A bit

later I remember to steer. A piece of cake. A pissy piste.
Listen to my *scales*, Kaki: Louis MacNeice's little fish,

little *fishes*, circling the first hurdle, the second rate.
The happy finish: each left fin wings its way to the inevitable right,

the inalienable right bestowed upon those who ask more than once for applause,
entitling everybody to exit through the big black backstage doors.

Matthew

poetry's part of your self
(Frank O'Hara)

or a gift from God. God's gift to you might be that you are God's gift.
The message on mý T-shirt makes that T seem more a crucifix:

I SPILLED MY GUTS FOR YOU PEOPLE AND ALL YOU GAVE ME WAS THIS.
See, not to show off but I grew up enjambing the two parts of the confess-

ional. My mind a grille. What goes in one ear comes out 'Mother,
I am stranded here on one side of what I think is a river,

and could never forgive myself for failing to be the leader
of men from the supercontinent to the isle of alders.' The grille is a ladder,

and although that grass might not be greener I am somebody who believes
us all entitled to believe ourselves laid upon its leaves.

I can tell you can tell I am very well informed. I write no sonnets;
do not attempt to second-guess me. For 'no sonnets' read 'one sonnet':

otherwise what hope in explaining the beautiful
woman's being beautiful like a bridge is beautiful?

[Part I]

Aubade

So sad. The sun stops giving the horizon head,
and rises... What a place to raise children. Or the dead.

Once risen they'll remark on time's grains of digital sand.
Querulously. But for now let such complaints be banned

– he said, imperiously. But seriously. For now take my fingers for torsos,
those of corpses trampled by steeple-chasing horses

and needing to be washed, cradled. For they're unable
to leave you thus uncoupled by the bedside table

beside the bed, unmade: they've read in your palm a mass
grave, its lifeline built on a fault line; a maze

in a killing field. How brave we are! How brave!
How saved! I pour my grave into your grave.

Any more equal and we'd be a minus.
Any sort of sequel would be an unwanted kindness.

Let us not seize the day by which we'll soon enough
be seized; let us forget how to breathe;

let us be motionless in our emotional urgency.
Let's not yet see, as if coming around mid-surgery,

the parting-poem blur between our eyes like a scalpel,
feel its downward drag like the tree in the apple,

or have it tip off the tips of our tongues like the nipple
towards which, fingers locked, we might appear to grapple

as we pray to the trickster Christ of the Infancy Gospel.

This clasp is the chapel. These digits the steeple-chasing people.

[Part I]

The Morning

I have plumbed the icy depths that you were probably saving for breakfast.
Fridge magnet haiku | twig in a block of winter | says you're the bestest.

A later sunbeam will key through leafsmoke: life will roll around it.
Now everything's locked. Three times this week I knocked the bedside

lamp from its perch; thrice it touched down as on down, its egg-brain unblown.
However devoted, however prepared, I expect I'd return the hijacked plane,

to say nothing of the passengers, in at least slightly improved condition.
The excrement I've slung is admired for its range and its shine.

The whiff of subtext. Sorry, that was me. It just happened.
It came from the other place. The place where my pitchfork bent

almost to snapping against the teeth of your chimpanzee smile.
Now to apply it to this most important meal.

The honey pilfered by rainclouds. The bulbs in one basket: the bird-hoard.
Who listens to 'I love you'? Those who, to believe, need not hear it.

Rhyme

The early bird catches something nasty.
The scaly-foot snail says, 'You do not mess with me.'
The Lord did not say, 'Should the right syntax oppress thee,
go pluck thyself.' This was left to the snail, as we see.

You do not mess with the scaly-foot snail
because it always speaks a slime-trail of truth.
The heights of martyrdom are what it scales.
It scatters gibbet crossbeams, shatters the roof,

says that on each screwed flower each white petal
is a wah-wah pedal, each martyr-dumb note a wah-wah-wah-
wah wonder. The early bird can't keep up.

The scaly-foot snail gives the early bird hiccups.
When seeming still, it does not stay but goes centripetal.
The early bird doesn't get it. The snail goes nah nah nah.

Form

Should you make too much love you'll have the rest
in sandwiches tomorrow. God takes the very best.

He takes his form at last. The form of grapes,
pressed for time and running like how fire escapes.

Milky little schoolgirl, strawberries and dream, cream
filling in a case of cream, I'm well aware of how it seems:

even if this pool of *fromage frais* could bone up to a fist,
Jesus would never want me for a New Formalist

– I don't do 'we'. And I'd ask you to join me, but, well.
Democracy is hell. Instead let's argue through a wall.

Your friends haven't done anything new lately.
And I'm your best friend, evidently. For more, see

the buttocks in the butter churn, the churn-stomaching mess where
I dropped an anvil, horn first, on the sleeping hare.

A Savage Breast

And so again the best words in their best order
have all the draw of a rock recorder

solo. All the impact of jellybeans
fired from slingshots at advancing US Marines.

All the fun of a sawn-off see-saw.
I flaunt a white flag like a white coat: a miso-

gyneticist committed to making things worse.
Second verse more cursed than the first.

I tut and tut and say you look like rain.
I touch a nerve. You tap a vein.

I probably think this thong is about me.
It absolutely isn't but it might be.

It absolutely is and that's what puts me off.
All your love's in vain. Why isn't that enough?

Sneer Poem

It's near enough.
You are the only one I love,
and other poems. *New and
Selected* has one wond-
er what the new ones did.
A hoop jump. A handstand.
Seeing the mess hall in this mass hallelu-

jah makes me want to tell you
you ought to be hospitalised
for your big brown hospital eyes.
Bleach – shit – death. So little
light do I provide that in the middle
there is no detectable glint.
This is what I meant.

Junk

a planet's encouragement
(Wallace Stevens)

The world as medication. It's becoming an addiction.
Where there's leisure for the coral reef, there's no need for fiction.
But it's not about need. My nurse provides suction.
She wields limpets limpidly. Her lucid affection!

She ought to be sectioned. One section, two.
Meiosis for me. Nothing for you.
There's nothing to do. I do it for cash, man.
Women take action. So sue me, Sue.

The glue of the gloom makes my motions slow.
My nurse was once nurse-scented jetsam. She'd float.
She'd block out the light. Now she butters my bones.
I do think it best that the devil rays know.

The jellyfish spread on the sunken dream.
Policing the polyps makes somebody mean.
Nothing is lost that can't be re-killed.
The world as medication. Prescriptions as landfill.

Lyric

disturb not her dream
(Robert Burns)

Once written, twice I
 – inevitable – and once halved one
might as well continue. Try
setting it to 'Sweet Afton'

of a mild evening. Get thee
into the vehicle! Witness ye
my dance – I am the lord, said he.
Be stunned by this my chassé.

I put the ass in chassis
when I enter. You're the in in winter.
So stick thee to thy lifestyle choices:
hang I at the dead centre,

self-landscape on a concave moor.
Am I the weight of your world?
The mooring-pegs ache at the corners.
It's by these, once quartered, I'm courted.

Phantom

Walking as through tundra. Untrue land.
We hug against the smug wind and we speak
of fire, and fucking pigs. While holding hands.
I think it might be nice to be a pig.

Ta-daa. Of such things one is not to speak.
And one is not to wrench thus for the metre.
You count its toes like so: 'This little pig
is guilty only of *attempted* murder,

this merely of consuming its own meat;
this third one of misapprehending Orwell.
This fourth obeyed a plausible lack of order.
And this one weighed its home against a pearl

and cast home pitwards...'
                                    Lash me to the wheel.
I need to know the swell, the strain. – *Oh hear*
us when we cry to thee | for those in peril
on the sea – A sea of freeze. A spear

between the ribs. Your heft of breath. I hear
the ring at the end of the note. I raise a hand
a touch too late, as if conducting pierced,
as if this treeless north were woodwind-lined.

A Complete History

The river is unabridged. So on its plane or plain
the plane crash-lands. The plane-crash lands. And Amazons amass
on its wing. They're not meant to be caught in the rain-
forest and yet here they are. It's dark. And yet, not to be crass,

that apparent half-absence, that famous mass mastectomy, misses,
apparently, not even half its mark. Their mastery
of 'Mystery Train' is second to none, these Ms-es
who string their bows and guitars

with, as it happens, lines in the sand.
As they breach the cabin the Amazons recommend
that all passengers interested in a change of attitude

purchase, and develop an appreciation
for, *Summer of the Whore, Horse Latitudes,*
Prozac Nation and, where available, the hits of The Sensations.

Deadication

Lee Perry's piss destroys his enemies. My kiss, at best, enjoys your canapés.
To work up appetites we race the stairs, which win, up to the canopy.

One of my more forgettable teachers kept it, memorably, simple,
said a great many species live there and monkeys are just one example.

A good example. Would that we were. Given that we're living here too.
I tremble in the wet air, and crush a rare ant beneath a mere toe.

Its death rattle: *You have fatted yourself on the deep-fried wings of your guardian angel.*
You value none above your own survival... That's rich, coming from the jungle.

I will never be rich, and the temperature is falling. O my ice cream cone!
I burn my very body for you! The very body of somebody I own!

A great ape sweats palm oil to grease my waistcoat's wasted pockets.
Saying as much seems to have helped. See this pocket watch? Watch it:

it's summing up the years I'll take to shake to sheer effluvia.
A gasp of invisible ink. With which something might be proved to you.

Badge

Mama, take these nails out of my actual *face*.
I won't be the moon's hushed-up Cenobite phase,

a goth Christingle or phantom porcupine embossed
on the star-slate. (Black spot's negative; the paste-

pot, dropped. An IED of chalk. A spatter of silt;
a skidmark of salt.) I was merely the first available slot.

Now I'm a board for the pinning of thoughts. A shaman
I was, sight-seeding, keening. I flinched. I saw a bunch of demons.

I led them out of Egypt. I said my name was Lesion.
But I meant to say Eejit. But they told me they were freezing.

Their pleas were somewhat pleasing. Tell me, mama, how it's kosher
that my blazer's basal buttonhole's a raw red rasher,

or that the long hog's grown up to be a freebaser,
truffling roast insignia with a pomegranate chaser.

Animal Testing, Testing...

The satellites of love are at half power.
And charging. Oink. This isn't war, it's race
hate: listen, what we need is plenty space.
Like castoffs – blastoff! – of the water bear,

these satellites are in their element
where elements themselves would fare with dread.
If only slightly differently attired
we'd pass from distance for one planet mooned

to excess. Exes claim as much. Our axis
that tilts so far we make rotisserie
appear a pole dance... *c'est la vie*. It rocks us

to sleep as sound as great big rocks. Quite sound.
Our mutters are the sound of history
compelling piglets over mine-mined ground.

Anselm Kiefer: *Laßt tausend Blumen blühen*

Many a despot may hang in his place of work. Many may not.
The justest obstruction still jams in the craw. Art sure does cost a lot.

Its charges, irreversible; its mighty, mighty charms. This time
it's personal. The lion lies down in your arms. Its steam

gets in your eyes. You look at each other with wilting surmise.
Every ruddy body cries. Weeps. The lion has shares and their price

is steep. A little garden, post-meridian, the earth a certainly fertile
vermilion... The bean-counter revolutionary stalks. Into the fairytale

tangle his brute is birthed. It blurts out bloodily. Birds sing
the Boss. Come on in and cover me. Everything *is* worsening,

Chairman, but then you must have known such a shade would make men
notice you. It's how you pay. It's what they do. When a rosebush is shaken

down, flower into frame corrupts. Proclaiming the non-endurance of power
may betray that power endures. The law of the thicket has many a lawyer.

Life in Stolen Moments

I

Although atop the motte I am heir to the air-built castle,
       they do call it a short swift slide from the mound of Venus to the asshole.

II

I would dig like a dog to bury this bone-parcel
       and grow something back to life from the germ of its own fossil.

III

Or set the skull to sea as its own vessel,
       its self-portrait wrapped around the wind like a muzzle.

IV

This is a day if ever there was one to wrestle
       with the dead things' commitment to the promised razzle-

V

dazzle of elsewhere. Here in the flavourless sizzle-
       free land of the living one might puzzle

VI

over the taste involved in the scratch and scrawl of trees' brown-dry bristles
       and wonder if the picture they press is worth the hassle,

VII

were it not for a sky so close being less a canvas than an easel
       against which this ellipsoid leans, pinned by pylons and seagulls.

[Part I]

Art Forsaking Art

The graveyards back onto allotments here
and there. The cattle mourn the pastoral.
Their lowing is a kind of high: it thrills
the currents of the air. Young leaves it wor-

ries. Rising godlike with fists full of throat
as train wrecks plot their figures on a graph.
I don't identify with sociopaths.
It doesn't take a lot to get my goat.

The slavery museum in Liverpool:
a crude ceramic favouring abolition
is seeking thanks for having stayed its hand.

Its simple generosity seems failed.
Upon the sunshine, questions fall. Aspersions.
The sleet is also culturally determined.

Kid

She threw you out to wander in mudfields guttered
by four-by-fours, in the attire of a goatherd
as you thought it, all coarse hair and sackcloth gathered

from bombsites. Eating insects and birds. You muttered
to the goat's-cheese moon of feeling stepped on, murdered,
of missing milk and butter and being mothered,

as if hooves like yours couldn't be clasped together,
or as if butting your stump-horned head into a puddle mattered.

A Fit Against

The left hand knows what the right rear leg wants.
The centaur's cento splices *Black Beauty* and *Frankenstein*.
He likes to correct people, tells them Beauty's
the name of the *scientist*, actually. Gulping
horse at the head end means he pumps
out hay at the arse. 'Hay pressed-o!' he shrieks
to nervous applause. Oh for some bolts, oh

for a bow. But he's no Sagittarius, no. Half
Libra, half Gemini: a tough couple of births.
He rarely remembers which came first
in the Year of the Second Opinion.
It isn't immensely important. His lovers
feed him sugar lumps or are arrested. Twilight:
a coin-spinner guillotines tiny sandwiches.

Blues for Marnie Stern

Before I woke this morning, I dreamed I rose by any other name.
Poetry's a preoccupation. I bought a new edition of the waiting game.

No dice. A shame. The single-sheet rulebook is missing a page.
Now I'm stuck exchanging puffs and puns with the watchful chronophage.

Its face is stocked with tics. To break it would be tygers burning Blake,
would be the book begging the self-publisher for *edits*, for heaven's sake,

would be the reciprocation of the love that seeketh wealth to please.
There's no time not to know your place. I smoke the breeze.

The chronophage smokes signals. Signet rings float on the river like, like, like cygnets.
Is that... is that right? *What value do yóu see in it?*

That's hard to say. The causeway's arm extends through mist, cattle, fox;
every drag rattles the bone-bag of the gear-shifts, the saddle, the padlocks.

'I' is what goes on without me. 'Marnie Stern': the stethoscope drilling my chest.
It's not my heart rate but my listening speed that has of late increased.

Sijo

I

Lover, the years have fine timing, or fine luck, I've noticed:
an old one dies, a young one stumbles mumbling onto the stage.
There will come a time when the new year is held back, firm by the wrist.

II

And, lover, consider the running down of the strong stag,
its only hope to lead the quick spear into the subtle mist.
You strike flint to raise a good fire. I tally days with snowdamp sticks.

Wednesday

Another day of fresh cigarette burns,
not failing to hit the side of a barn

but falling far short of a neat bull's-eye.
Not quite seeing the wood for the balsa,

knowing the great hereafter for elsewhere.
Athlete's foot, Achilles' heel, mouth ulcer;

one for the stomach, two for the money.
Nothing to see here. Give me a minute.

At the slow end of a forty-day fast,
peel peeling digits from your onion fist

and mask yourself with the pocked palm's odour,
the musk and slip of six weeks' work, either

mustard gas and ether or your man's flesh
flash-fried, seasoned, laid out, sprinkled with ash.

Refine

I would be crude. There is a fly in the ointment filming the camera lens,
and the day chained in the chamber of the eye or viewfinder
is sprung from its bonds with a suggestion of thunder
as the black cloud of the black box flashes, but this is all in silence;

all in silence, the process of the winter scene being unmade anew.
Distracted by a dissection of wings and compound eyes,
what could be less pure than this refraction of a billion days
into a white light's single abstract, and who seeing it now

could ask for better than this overdrive of cobweb and brainstem,
the crazy-paving of the world as it is, the sproutings of honeysuckle
and the constellations of firework and pinprick? Must we be metaphysical?
This snow is no quilt of quiet, but the silver discharge of a feedback system.

The Bone Fire

Well-dressed good-time guys and dolls caught *in flagrante*,
hot under the collar in the land of plenty,

dusting the body of the bone fire for keepsakes,
keeping our insides warm with swigs from a hipflask.

You discarded a dog skull, its tongue black ribbon,
and dug deeper, settling on a horse's thighbone,

which you'd use for a year as splint, taper, poker,
a ward against death, a sword put through the Púca.

The good pickings were gone when at last I plucked up
my fledgling feathers and put it in my pocket:

a small claw that crooked too much like a man's finger
for comfort. It thrummed at my thigh, warm nail-ember,

and I trekked to the heart of a conifer wood
and scratched your name, birthing smokestumps and loud fireweed.

II

What shall he have that killed the deer?
His leather skin and horns to wear.
Then sing him home; the rest shall bear
This burden.

Poem

Instead of the lily, consider the *Crocus*
longiflorus, think on its star or blue windmill
of David and the hotter droplet drawing-pinned
to its heart or throat, and act the better vandal,

drop-kicking a good handful of its pursed-lip seeds
with purpose across the clean white sheet of a wide
green field, where they'll nuzzle and knack at the soil's cracks,
guests wrecking the guest-room bed; later, at home, sit

alone, where nothing remains to be grown or said
– angels dancing, weightless, in a Zippo lighter –
and ease off your muddy boots, your feet still inside,

and purge your gorge of its trite Blind Willie Johnson
burr, devote the still-life evening to chancing
your arm at de- and restringing the old guitar...

A Resounding Success

You were restringing it, her father's guitar,
given to him years ago by her mother
and never played, passed on to the daughter
and intent upon fading into the ether
but now being dragged back to its metal and
wood. Its classical tastes asked for nylon strings,
and for a delicacy of touch to which any talent
you had was ill-fitted, carved more to the ring
of three steel chords, of a blues turnaround,
of the approximate or other authenticity.
The shared recognition was tacit:
you could do only so much. Perhaps it rained
that night as you two rhymed like twin tines
of a tuning fork, the guitar abandoned and still out of tune.

GDAE

My pursuit of you is more the pursuit of an even remotely acceptable
mandolin sound than it is the pursuit of something truly fleeing:
more the standstill of poetry than the stroll of prose, unstable
like the Tree of the Knowledge of Good and Evil, its freeing
of minds accomplishing something unrelated to progression. An apple,

I think, for your thoughts at this moment as the strings run their course,
as they run out of steam on this their steam-powered treadmill,
bruised apple-red and leather-black like the pump, the source
of all that keeps me going that I cradle, not sleeved in chain mail
but bare, lazy, open to the note you might find once we have spoken ourselves hoarse.

The Art of the Poetic Line

If the wolf-cub clouds clumped for warmth on the sky-like heather
are an excuse for opening with an observation about the weather
I walked in this afternoon, then the later chimney sweep's broom of
crows endeavouring through the sunset's pumpkin glow to remove
the blockage of shed wolf hair, by way of perpetual circular
motion, from the towering hollow between the coal-coloured
motorway and the ozone dome must, surely, be seen
as a sight for which memory was made. The crows, I mean:

there was something in their refusal, despite all else, to be end-
stopped that made theirs a state of impossible aspiration,
the best I can hope for being the justified placing
of my hand near yours, something upon which a little must depend.

Cold Turkey

Can't see no sky
(John Lennon)

We regret to announce that your flight has been delayed
by this announcement of regret. Calendars featuring the anal
passages of today's cabin crew must be paid
for. The hot chocolate isn't slow. It's special.
Satirical sonnets on this or any other airline
must go over your heads or under the seat in front
as the risk of becoming bad observational
comedy is high at this festive time. Friend
me. Do it now and I'll sell you a scratch card, and a penny
will go directly to an organisation that dispatches
aid to TINY CHILDREN scratched by scratch cards. They can't sell matches
for a very good reason. 'Tisn't the season. For want of smoke or any
snow everything else thaws. Why am I not surprised?
I close England and think of your eyes.

On Balance

The boy's voice is an arrow pointing upwards.
(Caitríona O'Reilly, 'Duets')

He wanted to know how to sing.
He was directed to geysers
and examining the rings

of muffled trees, treating them as notes
towards unity and range.
The disparate. The mutual.

He ate breadsticks, blood sausage,
bamboo. Daily he shinned
up ropes, stuck snakes with javelins,

hit things where they hurt; and nightly
he lay in his dirt
with his hands on his heart

forming an arrow or cross.
And he practised angling his neck,
so that in some impeccable chorus

someday, while he shouldered
the dull corner
of the harmony, he might look to the balcony

where the angelic soprano
would be equally a daredevil
fired from a cannon,

and base as he was he would play the game
straight, would not think it a burden,
this head-balanced jar, this stigma.

Dragon Foal

4 March 1982

Such a distance to travel
on the basis of a blind roll
on unfriendly gravel,

Dragon Foal,
ladleful of pot luck,
the jack's shoal

fracking ova from the muck
of a dry ocean bed,
the pocket into which it tucked

a winning hand. Ahead
of the pack,
if you were bred

for food or sport we'd still hold back
forever, growing hungry, slow,
thinking something more might tack

its way along that lowest of low
tides, amid sapped whales
that lost their flow,

amid coral and sea snails.
How long we'd wait
to hear what tales

it had to tell you, myth-bait,
sprung lie; how subtly try
to determine its birth date,

rummaging through the eye
of its navel
for a loaded die.

Three Cuckoos

I

Pity the cuckoo. If not
the adult,
compelled by a node
that levels the tilt

of other lives,
then the plump young
ringer that leaves
a nest. For as long

as one might remember
it has been unwitting
child to unwitting parents;

now it numbers
the days until it grants
that state the status of the done thing.

II

Sound drums in wood,
tumbles through the woods,
comes to a head,
dies...

flies up, fall-borne.
This is cuckoo spring,
this the full brain
pressing

to the rim of the cup of the skull.
Sockets brim with wonder
at the heaped

evictees, outgrown, called
out. Bailings-out on scales unhoped
besiege the base of every tree.

   III

The cuckoo is a pretty bad
sonofabitch.
It watches you make your bed
then lies in it.

It sows its wild oats
in your rose garden,
and with one swoop of its
wing swaps a measure of molten

mass into your good china.
Drinking's ill-advised,
but thirst being thirst

you might yet take on the chin
a chill clump homing to roost
in your mouth, volatile, vast.

A Further Bat

for Rebecca Watts

Quotation doesn't cover it.
The summer's half-packed overnight
bag makes its case: unhoist,
slumped on this sliver of crust

in local lowlight, all unbothered.
A little crotchet, shadow-tagged,
frets a dusk-lute. *Take heed,*
take heed; you'll wake my mother.

Weather cocks itself in vain:
no empty chamber ever rained.
Cloud flusters like a judge's wig,

donning which the bat whacks
a tolerant
check-mark into the margin of the fen.

Aye-aye

I am a pupil of the moon. When I look into my teacher's one dead
eye I meet my image, the ghost of which I am the ghost. Were-I, were
I to reach out as if towards myself, holding my held gaze all the while, I would
see me reaching in return, fingers branching across space,
linking as a hyphen, a rigged bridge, a tripwire
tripping orbits, gravities, tidal pull. When facing in vain my face
I am fulfilled by all that I fulfil:

unworded impossible prophecies, deep in deep time. I must be self-satisfied
but am without delusions: I know that I am godless and the devil's censer-bearer.
Uncensored naked evil. Darkness-wearer.
In moments of heat I recall my other lives, burned
at stakes for all that is at stake in me. I act dumb. My song would be a slow fall.
I am a pupil of the moon. I repeat myself. I have learned
to show one guise, to turn away from view my rhyming side.

Vorticists off Earth Now!!

i.m.

Don't that shining moon look pretty, baby? Don't that bridge?
Don't stand. Don't stand. Don't jump, though. No. Rage,

rage, shining down through the trees. All the pretty babies
are fine as moonshine, the bathwater thrown from lunar seas.

I'm no expert but I seem to accumulate degrees. In which I wallow.
I'm no penguin but I live a life informed as if exclusively by Christian values.

I'm no chicken but I can't use the fire blanket as I haven't been trained.
I have made an elegy for myself. Whoopty doo. You fetch the poultry and

I'll teach you to suck eggs. Repeat the procedure for lemons. Heavens.
Through the hard-boiled mouthpiece of this coil Clarence Clemons

poured Clarence Clemons, who exploded like an interference
field from its bell. Belle of the ball, judge me by my appearance;

but Rosalita, light a little jumper so that in his plummet
from the bridge he might sky-write an exclamation point, might

never, in fact, go out tonight. All right!! I like to write 'song'
so that my poems never, in fact, have to sing. They just sing along.

And I like proving people I care about wrong. Their dreams. Their hunches.
And I like it when I too fail, go too far, although not of course as much as

I like the Doppler effect of the saxophone breaking
apart but still powering the meteor, the meteor taking

its key-swapping, toe-tapping time as it tries to avoid
a sour decline and pulls itself back, up by its sax-strap, to meteoroid,

dips again and rises, repeats to a metaphor, a sinusoid, which as well as a sine
wave is, as I have learned, a blood vessel. Which might be sign-

ificant, although it's anybody's guess. Hell hath no
fury. Up there is all the rage. Remember? If I can't, you might have to

jog your memory all over the map
as elsewhere that rock star tries for another and another and another and
                              another and another and another and another lap.

[Part II]

Broadcast

Christopher Hitchens, 13 April 1949 – 15 December 2011

The whisky's choking 'to your health'
mind-forges manacles of peat.
The irony escapes itself.
This morning, for its meagre part,

thin snow clung like a skin of seed
to sodden grass on serious earth
then passed away. I could have died
but that, in spite, I caught my breath.

And caught my breath. And saw the sword
than which the pen is mightier cleave
a quill along its spine. The goose

that slipped it slipped beyond the reach
of what an eye might, outstretched, send
to draw what faint light comes and goes.

Glasgow

No end to it, the slow bomb of ink or
liquorice weeping its heart out through dusk
and dive, my unskilled puppeteer fingers
shadowing the string or wire of your spine.
Glasses seeing eye to eye on your desk.
How long since your communiqué from Spain,
how long until we're too close for comfort?
Quite long enough, we, whispering, agreed,
glossing over the split glass of our fort-
une's mirror, the hairline fracture, the break
with the traditions we'd taken as read.
Mixed breath. Strange dawn, like snowfall on a rook.

I believe you slept, but I was awake
all night. Every night. An endless week.

Tale

The way you tell it, I might as well have peeked
through the bedside blinds after our first lovemaking
to check if some passing woman or boy seemed keen,
displaying, surely needless to say, an utter lack of respect.

I wonder if you realise that to a degree I fancied myself
Narcissus, not falling hopelessly for the slim dawn reflection,
but wide-eyed enough to see the need for caution,
the risk of tripping over my own feet in disbelief,

the importance of watching myself, minding how I went.
And I wonder how much of this is getting through to you, given
that you've never seemed a fan

of the whole story; given that you emergency-broadcast, like Echo,
the last thing you heard – the refrain of airwaves, 'Idiot Wind',
an utter lack of respect looping or tailing off into static.

Cradle Song

You would taste tamarind, and you would know
the leathery cool of whiskey, the give
of a door opened correctly; and now
and then, with only the slightest of coughs,
the wingspan of your heartbeat would increase,
borrowing the wind and skimming stones, once
cradled in the darks of olives, across
an impossibility of distance.

In-flight

I am among passengers awaiting re-entry
to the world beneath cloud level.
You are as a mermaid inspiring flute-
song, to the tune of suggesting that love will
shape the sunset into the hills of a far country

or a heavenward drizzle of pheromone.
The aeroplane hands us over like a bandaged child,
a thimble of ocean, a cup of light,
and I picture you not coyly seashelled
but scaled like the perfect balance of that half moon.

From in Here

i.m. J. S. Mullan

From in here the painting has the texture of brick,
and is blue as a window, sill and frame matte black.

Clouds make themselves known, brush flourishes, yellow wisps.
Sailing stilly on oil water colour, six ships.

Or half a dozen boats, a handful of smudges
etched into the wet that laps, draws, at their edges.

Look closer. Over the horizon and creasing
the view as its centre, a butterflied half-sun,

a flurry of tone, the friction-heat of an itch
being scratched, the blunt thumbnail track of a struck match.

Cornered, at rest, the foothills of your signature.
The image is light. Makes quite the picture. Out there,

beheld in truth, the tale told when anyone dies:
the tail, the trail, of golden white, building to the sunrise.

Apfelschorle

I rode up on one till the bubble burst
(Robert Frost)

The suns of the golden apple-bubbles windfalling upwards.
Daybreaking new ground. Fresh flesh-yellow brick. 'King Midas in Reverse'

in reverse. A gullet of gold! A gully. A valley of golden gulls.
A volley of apples the wings fling. Utter splash. We all grow gills,

lung only to be *Luft*. The horses are all seahorses; the sea-trees candelabras,
each apple a little wet lamp ray. The heart or core of the apple-blood: this arbour.

But what's harder than ardour? What, now? Breaks a bough; changes
what's changeless. A seahorse rewinds. I cannot rub the sight from my strangeness...

And after 'After Apple-Picking', what? The payback of labour.
Consuming what I take. Yes. No less. I take no more than I pay for.

So I'm not the guy to run with. And I wonder where you'll stay.
And what you'd want to stay for. Hay and apples, apples and hay.

Look your gifted stallion in the mouth. Hey. You're defeating your maker.
Please, Hippomenes, off your knees. Your date-rape drug's docked in your trachea.

Better to Burn Out

Better out than in, according to Neil Young,
who still can't quite unfasten that note, make it detach
from its string. Hence this sort of knelling.
He says you should sometimes aim for the ditch:

hence this feeling of veering, this switch
to feigned loss from feigned sense of control.
Night drive home. The universe slows to watch
you flicker, tire, covet the centre. I pick up your trail.

The scent of epic fail. Petroleum; too long awake.
Lavender, and terror you can't shake. I'm not
putting your scent down. Your wick
should be lovely as a long weekend,

and I would not have you sleep, or half. The half-asleep
Christian says it's fine to be a sheep
but it matters what you want a sheep to be...!
It never counts. And even rust never sleeps with me:

it stays alert, lugging schemes through dense hazard of mind,
and on stirring I'm urged to keep up. Ever-losing,
I'd claim nothing valiant
for this flocky stubbornness, nothing worth praising,

nor'd I call us angels, me and my ilk:
backseat drivers, fevered, patching absurd
half-protective gestures onto sheep's-milk
bedsheets, those our riven love will never dye.

Come

Come brioche, come briar, we make it to Cumbria.
Blood on the sheets. Something I'd rather leave
behind than find – meaning bloody sheets are like my bloody self.
I look down on my head's resemblance. Dartboard. Sombrero.

On cinnamon soil a farm cat gingers its blank belly.
The ghostly heft of famished heifers: *though your sins*
be as scarlet... Not heeding warnings today. I'm post-signs.
No newspapers is good. Holy is as holy does, pal...

What used to be right is now wed.
The sheep in their sheet-dresses, bullet-holed;
centuries of dark-muffled grasp-ache, here held.
The window is widowing. Her pane a migraine of white.

If snow be white, it's snowing. The flakes blush like shy men,
decline. Why then her breasts are done and dusted. Why then.

Dirge

for Jo

When you think about me, do you think: 'about seventeen'?
I'm as old as some hills. I'm alive with eyes. I'm the real thing,

a.k.a. the most convincing fake. The water it takes
to tranquillise me recalls, in its quantity, lakes.

Fish eat fish as flakes, while in my bigger tank I'm so
stuffed with my flaked skin my sinews are ceasing to show,

so sibilant with longing I'm background radiation,
that steady underglow. So ancient I forget the creation.

Notion will rise against notion, although we hate the idea; and
that ground opens up although holy is evident. But it's a lake's crater, every dent:

one facet lit better can be most convincingly faked by all matter.
It's faith, or whatever. (The latter.) It's seed, or whatever, that which we scatter.

Ashes make flashes on the sainted sand. We're singing
in the grains. We're ringing in the right sides of the wrong ones.

Down the Ringing Grooves

after Tennyson

I ain't saying she's a bonedigger. But by the moon in the doglight,
the fogbow... she robs your sea-grave. Why? God knows. (... Delete.

Behave. Be brave. Leave the gods to their every sparrow...) Spring!
When a young man's fancy lightly turns to something harrowing.

Spring, and the ways are narrowing: the crowds of wet, the currents of rot,
recede; flushed fen asserts itself against unflooding road,

and outlines ripen in the turned-up gleam's new focus.
That means: all life's on watch and guard. Inversion: my *operandi modus*.

Like a beast with lower back pains, though I say *the crescent
promise of my spirit has not set*, I cannot but resent

the ease with which the burial goods were dredged up
from the slush of the late year's descent, and the job

that I now have: pickaxing and C-4ing the scape's thick ridge
for the bygone against which she, seafarer, unknowingly brushed.

Muse

That's an ankle bracelet, yes, but you don't háve an ankle.
Or so it appeared, paddling as you were in the inkwell.

A fetter of correcting fluid I spied, and misidentified. I'd let
you walk all over me – you'd leave huge   ing indents –

but for this need to live out the meaning of my creed.
By sleeping in my feed. You must have worked hard

not to have heard of Billie Holiday before your mid-thirties.
I border on impressed. A strange fruit hangs just south of my knees.

Which is very low. Daringly so. Hence out I go, out on my limbs,
two of them, initially... *What, in an interim, winces and limps?*

ponders the Sphinx. An errant ibis climaxes in its nostril.
The punchline's cudgel's an iron bar. Who would dare cross it? Al-

one in my bed, and well fed, I get to the other side. On days
ladies die I set alight a black flag. This is for cowardice.

An Explanation

Kipling's big joke, or Aesop's lost fable:
the story of how man got the feeling,

deep down in his heart or gut, of falling.
As I have it he was sloshed on whiskey

and hoping for a pull at the sky's flask,
snatching at the odd coins in the sea's purse,

thinking them moon or cloud: a fish-cirrus,
a dripping wad of tangled lunar rock.

Or somesuch. Thing is, it was such a shock
when he noticed the mermaid-girl weeping

that, all but sunk, he confused the open
water with close grey beach, plunged at what else

but a rabid breach, this drenched drag-Alice,
senseless, wrong-sized, far from ineffable.

III

The horn, the horn, the lusty horn
Is not a thing to laugh to scorn.

September

The sparks fly upward. Then I'm born.
You haven't seen my like before.
This isn't quite a compliment.
The sparks no longer make the rent.

They're soon evicted. Some are hosed down.
This my mongrel-voiced proposal:
impenetrably nondescript,
let my mind no marriage admit.

Still friends are wed at Hampton Court,
of which I'm sent to give report
in quatrains, user-edited.
I try to speak in relatives.

It could be worse. That's a joke.
Sorry for mumbling. Sorry I spoke.
Sorry for my keen aversion
to, of a sudden, sundry persons.

Sundry persons [who?] are dead.
Or let the thought go to my head.
I let my head go to my liver.
My head's a girl. I can't forgive her,

although some godly might demand it,
saying Christ is even-handed:
even, once the hate's abated,
a fairytale's views on race get dated.

Brothers Grimm, come eat my heart.
The sisters of mercy have gone and depart-
ed – *pace, pace*, Leonard Cohen.
Pace about your patchy cabin:

I'll pace myself about my mansion,
note floodwaters' surface tension,
buoy my mark, enunciate,
but skim the script and come in late.

And come in bulk. And come in brine.
Yet businessmen won't dig my whine.
I may make something close to sense,
but write it down as recompense:

the genius of my best man-speech...
They say my grasp exceeds my reach.
I'll end up holding far too few
of what the farther-reachers do

and fisting in my palm the tiny
love-to-love I'd hoped behind me.
It tries to give up. I can't let it.
I try to kill it, but I pet it.

The flash mob of the wedding dance
plays victim to my circumstance.
Adam treads on what Eve sews,
as Stanley Moss gathers what Sisyphus rolls,

and once I've crushed sufficient people
I hash out *Autumn Sequel*'s sequel,
grow from my initials *hack*,
make beasts with a paperback.

I'm loaded now with crappy stew.
Commence the taming of the screw.
I have not one regret to give.
I've other people's lives to live.

I've crows to cock. I've ears to lop.
I long to make the Swedish pop.
My future's as a hoarder, sort of:
witness my canned-laugh-packed aorta,

and lick my love pump, Lykke Li.
My wiki leaks a lot of me.
I sell the farm. I sail the Main.
I worry 'bout the army in the slow, slow train.

Dawn

Dawn is like the dawn: thinks she's all instinct
and the world happening to her. Stuttering
frames mime her rising on the big screen
in her small mind. Small with many mansions.

When Dawn squeezes teabags they sprout berries.
When Dawn sneezes, buildings self-erase,
fall on the rising swords of their absence.
When Dawn is in the shower, the water pummels

only the air around her. The air around her
is where Dawn hunts the big game: the panther,
nightfall. She stalks the stalker. The rain slicks its fur

and it's now in her sights. Her eye is of the storm
on the eastern horizon. Her clouds: black mammoths that dream
of feeling panthers underfoot, kittens flattening into loam.

Caitlin Rose Knows

I was raised in Middle England, not in Nashville Tennessee
(Frank Turner)

Man, that's country. Let's listen to Gene Autry
and try for a second or third time this evening to forget
that despite the elections scuppered or rigged
we are far from the world's policeman, far from its janitor;

let's stare into the barrel of monkeys and ape-
ape- ap*prec*iate the situation in which we precisely don't
find ourselves. I would kill for my own rape
kit. I am cold from baring my arms. I'm a doughnut.

Tell me there's a single ingot we can trust.
Tell me that's blood on your hands, not rust.
Ah, love, let us buy shoes for one another! Try it
again, only this time with your tongue out.

Our songs are all sung out. Take my gun.
Seriously. That's not a joke, that's country, man;
the plans you've laid are the best I've seen. Who's gonna
want me when I'm just somewhere you've been?

You Are Superior

Plunge, and in vortex that destroys it, puppy,
Drink deep the imaged solid of the bone.
(William Empson)

wind ruffling through first feathers then fur
(Matthea Harvey)

I'm a flop-notch Knopfler knockoff. More easily said than denied.
There was a touch of lupine blood on my foster mother's side.
You can hear it in the way I sometimes howl along
in accidental harmony with ambient birdsong,
in how *all I do is kiss you through the bars of a rhyme*,
in how all you do is throw me right back into the cradle,
it not yet being kissing time. We must draw the line at cordial.

You draw a line in black at my waist's circumference and ask me why
I behave always as if precisely that high. What a bad boy
am I. If not for this wolf hair, I'd be a bad little bear;
there's something in me, honey. *I can't do the talk.*
I'm a sparrowhawk. I let you go to my head.
The little bird of my lover is dead.
The regression you've kicked off won't kick-stop at infant:

you are dealing right now with a child of the infinite,
giving me almost enough time to nail the famous intro.
It's been so long the very *in utero* of *in utero*,
the big bang in our respective guts,
that in the quest for the gut-dust we sometimes forget
that Mars enters into it no more than Venus.
We sometimes forget while we're gorging on locusts

that you are the Cybermen and I, love, the Daleks.
My eyestalk's awful phallic. See those trees? Big thrusting wood
but they're radical feminists. You have to stand for something. I mean this.
I'm sleek but you are better at dieting; should
you split me in two you'll find not rings but pentagrams.
Forgive me, but. We're in straits direr than Romulus, than Juliet.
I think I have it now. Leave it to me. Exfoliate. Exfoliate.

[Part III]

Kneel

The chapel pukes its shadow on the courtyard.
The shadow makes the opposite of profit.
Clearly more than I have, it's thought hard
on why the stain on stained glass won't come off it.

I avert my gaze and cough: self-employed fluffer
copping a feel of atmosphere funereal.
Lord, what did you have to go and *love* for?
I wanted to try out my new material.

Your holy hands come off in my holy hands.
I'll take the rear. I know where is an hynde
to render unto Caesar; I know where is a star,

a real down-on-your-knees-er, that far
outseizes you in matters of the day.
But bodies rise and people get carried away.

Zombie

All levity is how the sky feels.
Reverend breaks bread with revenant.
They agree on how Old Testament
morality, crowd-surfing in high heels,

will have somebody's eye out.
The sticking point is decision-making.
The reverend's all for saying the king
is undead and inciting a riot,

while his buddy's all about the wait:
'Take a load off, father,' he wheezes.
'And as for somewhere to lay it,

the sea of hands is not to be dismissed...'
(The larynx, losing it.) '... I mean, Jesus,
the most of them even have their fingers crossed.'

Cockatrice

It clucked, and spat at the best of both worlds.
The monster hatched by a mother-serpent
from an egg laid by a too-proud rooster
twisted copper about a girl's wrists, her
ankles, her throat. It squatted, watched her, penned
a tribute with a claw pisswet, bloodwhorled,

and badinaged with her would-be saviour
and caught his eye and struck him blind and dead.
A winged beast can be so underhanded;
its pupils were graves dug amid sapphires...

Of course its parents were disappointed
but still loved it. To test them it painted
over their scales or feathers as they slept
and rolled them howling down a rocky slope.

From the Lithuanian

for Ingrid

The clearest of visions demands filter after filter.
If you let the pig into the church, it'll climb on the altar;

turn it away and it learns how to curse. Some can barely
face the cadence of that third pint of Estrella

– this is what we talk about when we talk about loving talking.
With all we know of loss, with all we know of every token

syllable of English verse being but a fingernail-sized bird
once the petrol-puddle tongue's flung up its drunken parrot,

still we baffle at the half-assed *plop* as yet another frog jettisons
its ghost. The riverside pub a voice-activated complex. Lights, *on;*

bite down on the draught of plumage while I make my first incision.
To apply this wealth of filters demands the clearest of visions:

uttering something broken, unbuttoning its cutesy halter,
I let the pig into the church. I let it climb on the altar.

[Part III]

Pussy Rot

Long live the megachurch! People
have been hurt. In time forgive,
forgive. Forget in time. Stand stable
by convictions. Long live, long live.

It takes the I in riot to barge in
to the gangrenous harbour.
It takes more than balls to bargain
with the grin edging a dull sabre.

Pins of rain prick at some shore:
a cloud table unsettling its crumbs.
The approaching boat's figurehead

inflates about a breath of fresh air
through lips two Russian pogroms,
red and stained.

Crow Snow

Precipitation might have made it into the poem again. But where it should squeak
beneath the boots stamping on its face, forever, a squawk appears to take

the place of this and any other note of absence. A morbid jeer,
rather, rises, precisely like steam except for the obvious differences. A corvid year

is underfoot, soles on feathers leaving naught amounting to a track.
Any man made of this would be a quilled thing, tar-black.

Compacted it cracks like morning with a dawn chorus of insurmountable death.
Come in. Eat crow. Drink snow. Become a celebrity survivalist chef.

Those birds have definitely made it into the poem again. A mock-up
of your humble host, gown hung around the dropped sword of Damocles, telescope

eye poised on its hilt, has done nothing to dissuade them. It is unscary.
The synaesthete sins against definition. By definition. Something very

like snow wails. Your humble host undertakes, ever the clueless exacerbator,
to grind it out. The sky falls. Something will pick up the pieces later.

Dr Nelson's Improved Inhaler

Abstract seal pup,
scalp louse,
flayed echidna: there's an app-
endix come loose

from this milk tooth
hand mirror. Dr Nelson
took the oath;
was full of it. Tensions

heighten a little.
The cost of the corkage:
knowing the vessel's
a bottomless package,

white light white steroid
expanding unhindered.
You'd take it in your stride
but you stride like an insult.

Those who can, walk off
the slippage of image,
the potter's-wheel cough
in the egg of an ostrich,

water-gas farmed
from a last-minute unicorn,
alveoli charmed
by the amoebic flugelhorn.

Consulting the notes: beige
Art Deco sofa.
Conch *sans* texture. Taj
Mahal souvenir.

The harm in these meetings
'twixt padlock and keychain.
That membrane. Your hating
translating its freeze-frame

hack semaphore's flaws. Your
plainly not wanting the platinum
frond. Sip from its samovar:
your lip's snipped upon

the hilt of the sabre you plunged
through an astronaut. White-
face the fact of it. Blanch
the whole coconut.

Ray gun as hair dryer.
Albinised leech.
Bronchioles as samphire.
Those who can't, bleach.

Pale tapir of vapour. I want it
poured into me.
Breathe freely in and out
as if you were ordinary.

North

Tray tables rattle like teeth
in the mouth of train travel reportage.
A train ought not to match
the image of a funeral wreath.

But here it is. A circuit of sage
and onion. Wise, weeping, with-
ering. The relativity myth:
once you start thinking geo-

logically, none
of this will move.
Kick the stuff-

ing from me. Such is your training,
rolling rock tracks. Shake, of course. Rattle
my teeth like tray tables.

Overhang

I can't kaleidoscope with the shame in my rainbones.
The hangover poem blocking, petty, out the stars:
a drum-tight close-up of *La cour du domaine du Gras*
graining the eyeball militarily. Megaphones.
By 'stars' one means the mute infinity of the sun's
being *yariganna*'d into winding-sheet-slender
escalopes that rim, corona, this vast game-ender
that backs the body against all that stammers, hums, errs.

I Just Dropped In (To See What Condition the Human Condition Was In)

God is a concert, standing-room: you shuffle
to the front because tall people are evil.

Must you watch your life through a chancel
screen? I call you Betty, you call me Hansel:

the crumbs in my aftermath, gingerbread births.
Hear ye: *in their hands they shall bear thee*

up. Thumbprints on collapsed arches.
Bypass the ruin, you shoo-in. Enjoy the largesse.

Can entry be refused by those who enter?
Can paradise on earth come close to entire

when however much we machine-gun
the pregnant they still insist on bringing it upon

themselves? God is a precept, set
in stone as my hand-stamp. God's a receipt.

Villanelle Fire

A car explodes until we're all inside.
I only came outside to take the air.
I caught the gist of what the swallow said

(the swallow prides itself on lacking pride):
'For god's sake, get the kids into the car!'
A car explodes until we're all inside.

It happens all at once, which isn't bad.
A paranoid interpretation snares
'I caught the gist of what the swallow said'

and plucks its feathered shrapnel from my head;
I kiss you and I kiss a solar flare;
a car explodes until we're all inside.

You don't believe the day we would have had.
You don't believe a thing, though, any more.
I caught the gist of what the swallow said

and thought its payload was a heavy load
to bear when shuttling through a system where
a car explodes until we're all inside
'I caught the gist of what the swallow said'.

Open

your mind
is what the predator
is predicated on. You're
quite the find,

although the most
dangerous prey isn't
man but a veritable saint.
Verifiable. Best-

itality. A vulture
loves a bad girl.
A bad *gull*.
It wants to hold her

hand-
lebars.
Carc-
inogen

synergy is synonymous
with the vulture holding
its good little girl-thing's
handlebars like mice.

Mice aren't small fish
but you have to think about it.
Baldy guides his girl guide
on her new bike. Newish.

Swish swish goes the long
grass you mustn't go into.
The predator is predicated on the
girl guide's mind opening.

The poppy field is poppyless
but populous with poetry
words. It wrote the entry
on soporific gas.

It wrote the god damn book.
The vulture rode the bike
in his day. He would click 'like'
on a picture of the bike

but the most danger-
ous prey is verifiably in
the area, hiding in plain
cover. As is the predator.

The vulture will raise
what the predator leaves
when the predator leaves.
The leavings will rise.

The saint has been verified. Hard.
The vulture's head – unfeathered, nonetheless
tarred – seems to demand redress.
The saint, saintlily, feigns not having heard.

That the poem is hard is veri-
fiable; that it is heard, less
so. It will un- and re-dress.
Nobody knows its sorrow.

Most poems are bubbles.
This is a bubble wand:
insufficient, a lean-to
transmitting wakes of symbol

as if this tamed the chiasmus,
saved girl-thing, vulture,
predated saint or predator,
thickened no miasma.

Most poems are dead ends,
but this is as open
as an invitation
bookmarking a book of wounds,

marking the entry
where the book anyway opens:
a wound that will wait for its weapon
until mid-next century,

a weapon that is open-ended,
as, one might opine,
they all have always been.
The smallest is two-handed:

hand-me-down bike as
girl-guided missile.
Any other missive
is relatively closed, because

this is an open
letter to the open field. Gulls
circle. *Opium* field. Crop circles
and moves in.

Draining Song

Rain like a history of sonnets. Mud, overturned. The old flames
buried and by now so sweet they forget their own sweet names.

Or I do. Fall-apart time. Day-slide. Session of mists.
Sorely, very sorely, missed. What I'm saying is, there must

be a line between corrupt and corrupted.
I'm saying the local volcano has not recently interrupted.

I'm saying we stopped it. Politeness, like ignoring the night blindness
of the knight in shining pun whose perfect kindness

was to gather your panoply of woes, heave-ho, and throw
them, like so many cautions, at the closed window.

What stuck narrowed your options. Welcome to the club.
I tried to be grim with grace like Seidel and there's the rub-

ble to prove it. The grit. For old Rydell I shook a nyctalopic tit
and cheered on the rain whose sonnet is a history of it.

Blues for Katie Crutchfield

I believe I'll bust my doom today. The belief will be suspended.
The mantis prays for the *sac-a-lait*. The end of the world has ended,

and *Confessio Amantis* plays line fourteen – beyond which nothing – on repeat,
to celebrate. It comes through walls like spam. It dulleth ofte a mannes wit.

It whittles one down. The crappy crappie rejects the prayer,
but on it goes. It flays, it blows. Exit, pursued by a bore.

Give up on the stick figure. Throw me. I'll fetch me.
My portrait's a selfie. Side-on I see you. My profile is sketchy.

I don't have Waxahatchee Creek. I don't know the bite of an elk.
I barely know how to speak. I creak. My synovial fluid is malted milk.

This you should know: if you're tiring of trying, you're free to let go. My
doings undone from the get-go; my sleepy head; my coma

toes... My trail goes cold. My army of geckos lose limbs by the thousand.
I'm talking autotomy. It's something you taught to me. Take my hand.

Couplets

O little poems. Loitering always around my blind spot,
with pips in your grin-gaps and your flaps unzipped.

I shall, I swear, compare thee to the wind, that which winnows
the unlovely from my beloved. This comparison for the win.

Fork my life in a yellow wood, in your long and narrow way.
I'd better claim that the name of my game is Go Not Far Today.

Stricken and flayed. Miming a picket line. Air-fencing.
Reducing my antlered spirit guide to a pencil sketch of venison.

All skin and clone at this point, I buff my binding to shunt
my original sense out of sight. I worsen that tooth. I rip this joint.

Another dead white dude lost in a forest. The urbane
jangle of the twenty *memento mori* he's purloined.

His poor loins: ungirded, gone off-grid. Sat so long in lechery's
lap he ceased to want it. Ironical clap. Three cheers.

Clear as the kestrel that seemingly floats in his wrecked
left eye is the outlook. Debt is not the end. Every bird's an insect.

Every champion doesn't mind being thick. A trickle
of light petting obscures the sickle's glare. Red is every squirrel.

As for splatterbrain's caterwaul: variation on a theme
tune. Why aren't they screaming? Why can't I be more like them?

How might glow that so swells the grove be led to settle?
Can't write. Can't write. Slightly bald. Can write a little.

[Part III]

I write of Hell; I sing (and ever shall)
Of Heaven, and hope to have it after all.

Robert Herrick said that, teasingly. Can't he hear me
knocking heaven's storage capacity? I do. It ain't easy.

It's Adam and Adam, not Adam and Eve: *you're a big girl's*
blouse all the way. Let us bray. A reading from the Book of Heckles.

The first-line index opens with lengthening howls
that take up columns. *I* is not my favourite vowel.

My favourite language is volumes. I speak it. My picture's
worse than a thousand bad words. It's a lecture.

I give it to the trees that won't let me hug them. A buzz
as of a billion saws is all my audience is, or was.

Little poems, strike my pose. Observe me thus aloft: a trophy,
dribbling and dripping a rank primordial soup. The unquiet gravy.

Before the flies arrive you might wrestle me off this meat hook.
Don't bother. They're here. O little poems. O little book...

Go, little book. Begone. Be with me on my wedding night.
Our mutual revulsion binds our passions in its knot.

§

Notes

The section epigraphs are from *As You Like It*, IV. ii.

Phantom: 'Of Fire, and Fucking Pigs' is a song by Anaal Nathrakh.

Badge: This was written for a poetry competition at St John's College, Cambridge. Entrants were asked to write in response to items from the College Archives, among them a badge representing a pig.

Anselm Kiefer: *Laßt tausend Blumen blühen*: Kiefer produced several paintings in response to time spent in China, including a depiction of a statue of Chairman Mao largely obscured by dry twigs and flowers.

Sijo: The sijo is a Korean verse form. This poem is made up of two approximations.

GDAE: The title refers to the standard tuning, low to high, of a mandolin's four pairs of strings.

Dragon Foal: Dragon Foal was a hybrid animal, conceived by a female hinny (the usually sterile offspring of a male horse and female donkey) and male donkey (or 'jack') and born in China on 4 March 1982. Her genetic composition had not previously been documented.

Aye-aye: The aye-aye is a species of lemur, under threat in part because of superstitions pertaining to its not being conventionally attractive.

Vorticists off Earth Now!!: Cowboy Junkies' 1986 debut album, *Whites off Earth Now!!*, opens with a version of 'Shining Moon' by Lightnin' Hopkins.

From in Here: This describes a painting by my grandfather, to whose memory the poem is dedicated.

Dirge: The opening sentence repunctuates a line from Eric Church's song 'Springsteen'.

September: I actually had a lovely time at my friends' Hampton Court wedding.

Caitlin Rose Knows: The final sentence is from the song 'Own Side' by, yes, Caitlin Rose.

Couplets: In 'The Argument of His Book', Robert Herrick did indeed say that.